let's get down
to business

This book is dedicated
to all who wish to
turn their passions
to purpose!

Dream
Beautiful
Fly High

"Logic will get you from A to B.
Imagination will take you everywhere."
- Albert Einstein

Do you have a fulfilment outside of the day job, have an idea but don't know where to start? This book is designed to help you get off the starting blocks to plan and make your ideas happen.

There's no getting away from it, starting and running a new business or side gig is hard work, time consuming and, at times, stressful. However, it can be the most profoundly, satisfying and stimulating venture you may ever take!

Making your ideas happen to gain success is your utmost goal but it is also important not to overlook the outcome — how you are going to make it happen — rather than simply the process. This overlooks an important aspect— the possibility of having a HAPPY business.

The pages in this book are designed to make your ideas happen. From basic brainstorming, problem solving, budgeting, finding solutions and making choices to finally polishing them up to make them a reality!

What are you waiting for? Turn your passion to purpose ....

Create ....

"Someone's sitting in the shade today
because someone planted a tree a long time ago."
- Warren Buffett

Brainstorming

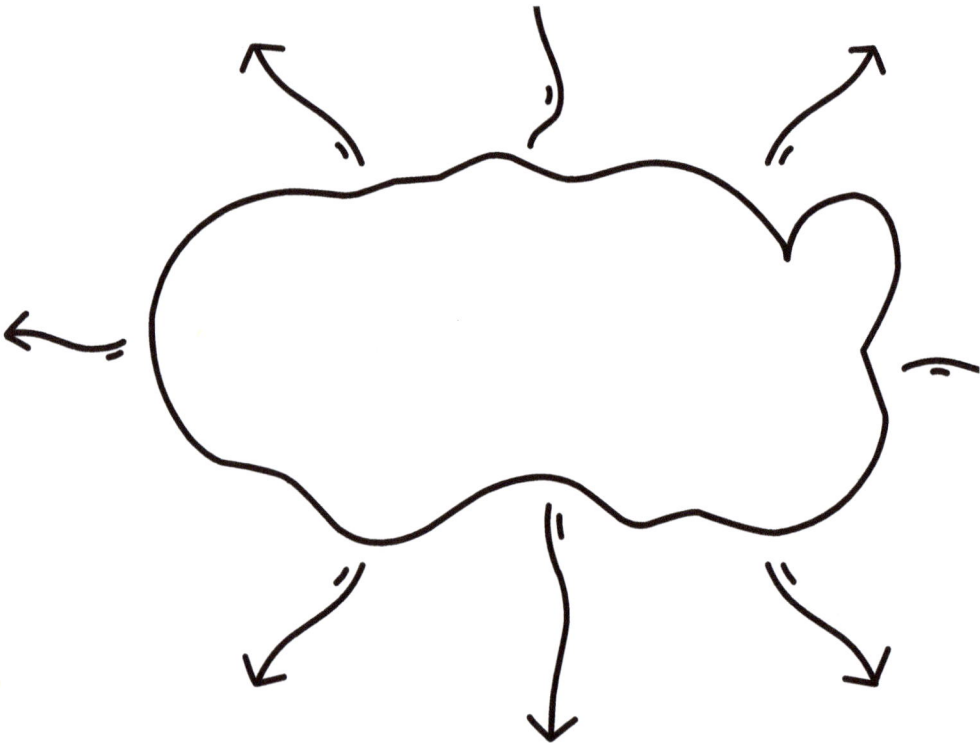

So you have your ideas and you now want to plan how these ideas can happen — how you get from A to B and then from B to C.

Consider the process — use your ideas to paint a picture of what you are aiming to create.

How will you sell your idea/product/service?
How will you tell the world about your business?
Who will be your customer?
What competition might you be up against?

Fundamentally, how will you get your idea out there?

Having ideas

PROBLEMS

PEOPLE

SOLUTIONS

CHOICES

PROBLEM

Don't fall in love with your idea, instead fall in love with the problem your idea solves. Fall in love with the people who have the problem and the customers who use your solution — they will guide you to a better idea!

PEOPLE

Connect with others – you need to keep connected to people as you build your idea. It's essential for you to talk to them and get feedback – how else will you know you're creating something people want?

SOLUTION

To find a good solution you need to have lots of ideas.

Write a 'How might I ....? question and draw a mindmap to stimulate your creative thinking.

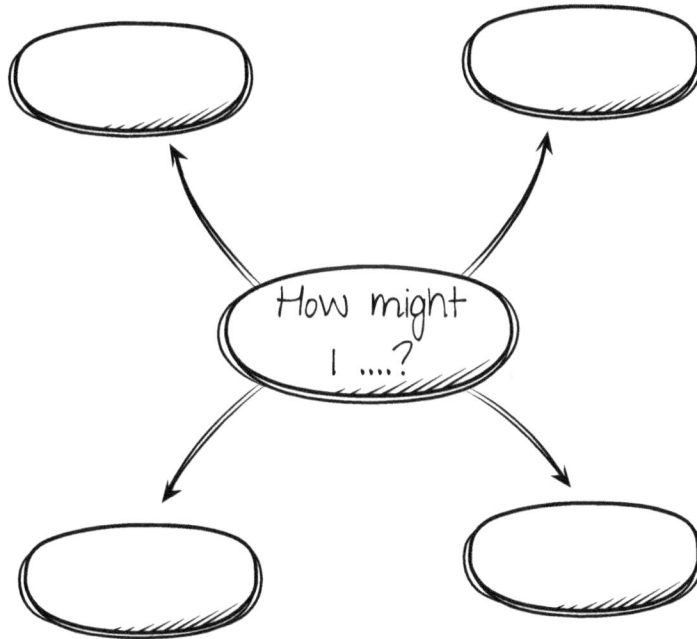

How might I ....?

CHOICE

While it's great to have multiple ideas, we can get overwhelmed deciding between them. This can result in becoming less likely to make a decision when there are more options available. It is also known in some cases to feel burdened by the responsibility of distinguishing between good and bad choices.

A good first step in making favourable decisions is to define criteria. Grab some paper and write a list of no more than six criteria. Then draw up a chart or grid listing the ideas against the criteria. Create a scoring system and go through each idea and score against the list. Finally, tally up the scores and you'll have a winner!

DECISION MAKING

FOLLOW THE PROMPTS BELOW TO BRAINSTORM SOLUTIONS TO A DECISION YOU ARE FACING. CHOOSE THE BEST SOLUTION BASED ON YOUR ANSWERS.

WHAT DECISION ARE YOU TRYING TO MAKE?

	ADVANTAGES	DISADVANTAGES	CONSEQUENCES
SOLUTION 1			
SOLUTION 2			
SOLUTION 3			

THE SOLUTION I CHOSE AND WHY

_____

_____

_____

Goals

Put it into Action

LOVE WHAT YOU DO
Start a business in a product or service you love and will enjoy.

HAVE a BUSINESS PLAN
Know how you are going to create value. Be able to be articulate what you are producing, buying and selling, to whom and, at what price.

Goal
SETTING

START DATE: __/__/____   END DATE: __/__/____

MY GOAL IS ...

MY WHY	TO REMEMBER

ACTION STEPS

- ☐ _____
- ☐ _____
- ☐ _____
- ☐ _____
- ☐ _____
- ☐ _____
- ☐ _____

THINGS TO USE

- ☐ _____
- ☐ _____
- ☐ _____
- ☐ _____
- ☐ _____
- ☐ _____
- ☐ _____

DRAW / SKETCH

GRATEFUL FOR

" "

Goal
SETTING

START DATE: __/__/____   END DATE: __/__/____

MY GOAL IS ...

MY WHY	TO REMEMBER

ACTION STEPS	THINGS TO USE
☐ _____	☐ _____
☐ _____	☐ _____
☐ _____	☐ _____
☐ _____	☐ _____
☐ _____	☐ _____
☐ _____	☐ _____
☐ _____	☐ _____

DRAW / SKETCH

GRATEFUL FOR

"
"

Goal
SETTING

START DATE: __/__/____   END DATE: __/__/____

MY GOAL IS ...

MY WHY	TO REMEMBER

ACTION STEPS	THINGS TO USE
☐ _____	☐ _____
☐ _____	☐ _____
☐ _____	☐ _____
☐ _____	☐ _____
☐ _____	☐ _____
☐ _____	☐ _____
☐ _____	☐ _____

DRAW / SKETCH	GRATEFUL FOR

"

Goal
SETTING

START DATE: __/__/____

END DATE: __/__/____

MY GOAL IS ...

MY WHY

TO REMEMBER

ACTION STEPS

- [ ] _____
- [ ] _____
- [ ] _____
- [ ] _____
- [ ] _____
- [ ] _____
- [ ] _____

THINGS TO USE

- [ ] _____
- [ ] _____
- [ ] _____
- [ ] _____
- [ ] _____
- [ ] _____
- [ ] _____

DRAW / SKETCH

GRATEFUL FOR

"
"

Goal
SETTING

START DATE: __/__/____   END DATE: __/__/____

MY GOAL IS ...

MY WHY	TO REMEMBER

ACTION STEPS	THINGS TO USE
☐ _____	☐ _____
☐ _____	☐ _____
☐ _____	☐ _____
☐ _____	☐ _____
☐ _____	☐ _____
☐ _____	☐ _____
☐ _____	☐ _____

DRAW / SKETCH

GRATEFUL FOR

" "

Goal
SETTING

START DATE: __/__/____   END DATE: __/__/____

MY GOAL IS ...

MY WHY	TO REMEMBER

ACTION STEPS	THINGS TO USE
☐ _____	☐ _____
☐ _____	☐ _____
☐ _____	☐ _____
☐ _____	☐ _____
☐ _____	☐ _____
☐ _____	☐ _____
☐ _____	☐ _____

DRAW / SKETCH	GRATEFUL FOR

66

99

My

Plan

MY PLAN

Turning passion to purpose — can you envisage your ideas painting a picture of what you're creating? This process makes you think, the more you think, the more you will challenge yourself and your ideas.

Some final thoughts .....

Thiink about how will you tell people about your business?

How will you sell what you've created?

In a nutshell, how will you tell the WORLD about your business?

MY PLAN

Customer – who is your customer? what competition might you have?

Cost – how much will your product or service cost? what price do you need to sell your product or service in order to create profit?

Skills – what skills are you bringing to your business or will you need to hire or outsource help?

Don't forget you – what will you charge for your time?

PUT IT INTO ACTION

Love What You Do

wALK yOUR oWN pATH

UNDERSTAND YOUR CASHFLOW .....

One of the most important aspects of any Business is keeping track of financial performance.

Consider how much money you may need to get started. Have you understood the costs?

Now is the time to plan well in this area of your business.

Start Up Costs

No	Item (s)	Cost
1		
2		
3		
4		
5		
6		

- Notes

_____

_____

Start Up Costs

No	Item (s)	Cost
1		
2		
3		
4		
5		
6		

- Notes

_____

_____

INCOMES & EXPENSES

MONTH OF

INCOME	CATEGORY	AMOUNT
		TOTAL

DATE	EXPENSE	CATEGORY	AMOUNT
			TOTAL

INCOMES & EXPENSES

MONTH OF

INCOME	CATEGORY	AMOUNT
		TOTAL

DATE	EXPENSE	CATEGORY	AMOUNT
			TOTAL

REFLECT

_____

_____

_____

_____

_____

_____

_____

_____

_____

_____

_____

_____

_____

_____

_____

" *We do not need magic to change the world, we carry all the power we need inside ourselves already. We have the power to imagine better.*"

- J. K. Rowling

REFLECT

_____

_____

_____

_____

_____

_____

_____

_____

_____

_____

_____

_____

_____

_____

_____

_____

"True leadership stems from individuality that is
honestly and sometimes imperfectly expressed... Leaders
should strive for authenticity over perfection."
- Sheryl Sandberg, COO, Facebook

REFLECT

_____

_____

_____

_____

_____

_____

_____

_____

_____

_____

_____

_____

_____

_____

_____

"All our dreams can come true, if we have the courage to pursue them."

— Walt Disney

PUT IT INTO ACTION

The Weekly Reflection

Walk your own path — generating success and wealth means doing things YOUR way. Experiment, take what's good, build on the ideas and habits you like and ultimately, tailor and tweak things to better you, your needs and situation.

This helpful tool is designed to reflect as you begin to build your business journey .....

Your WINS — reaching your business targets, achievements, new contacts, etc

Your CHALLENGES — the things that have got in the way or outside of your control. These challenges often turn into reflections.

Your LESSONS — there will always be an opportunity to learn!

Your FOCUS — for the week ahead. This should ideally be linked to your vision.

The Weekly

REFLECTION

WINS	CHALLENGES
LESSONS	FOCUS

The Weekly
REFLECTION

WINS | CHALLENGES

LESSONS | FOCUS

The Weekly
REFLECTION

WINS	CHALLENGES
LESSONS	FOCUS

The Weekly
REFLECTION

WINS	CHALLENGES
LESSONS	FOCUS

The Weekly
REFLECTION

WINS	CHALLENGES
LESSONS	FOCUS

The Weekly
REFLECTION

WINS	CHALLENGES
LESSONS	FOCUS

The Weekly
REFLECTION

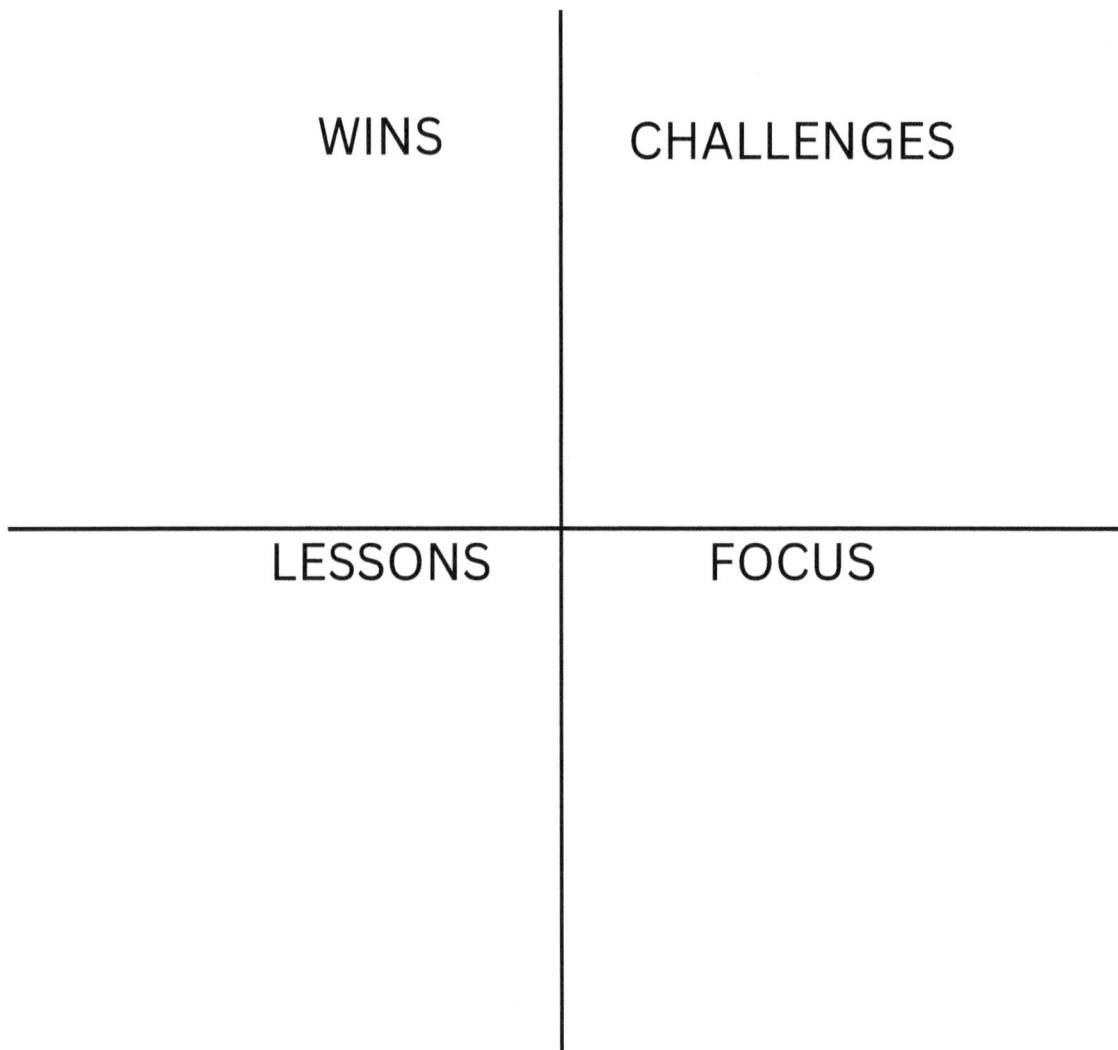

WINS	CHALLENGES

LESSONS	FOCUS

The Weekly
REFLECTION

WINS | CHALLENGES

LESSONS | FOCUS

The Weekly
REFLECTION

WINS	CHALLENGES

LESSONS	FOCUS

The Weekly
REFLECTION

WINS

CHALLENGES

LESSONS

FOCUS

The Weekly
REFLECTION

WINS	CHALLENGES
LESSONS	FOCUS

The Weekly
REFLECTION

WINS | CHALLENGES

LESSONS | FOCUS

Remember, this is YOUR plan and there is no 'right' way to build a business. Rather than a business plan, have a vision. This vision of what your business is going to entail and where you want it to go!

gOOD luck!

Creating and continuing your business journey

On the following pages you will find some helpful planners to help organise your days ahead as your business develops.

You may find it beneficial to make copies or adapt the pages to suit your own purposes.

DAILY PLANNER

TODAY:

Time	
8 AM	
9 AM	
10 AM	
11 AM	
12 NOON	
1 PM	
2 PM	
3 PM	
4 PM	
5 PM	
6 PM	
7 PM	
8 PM	
9 PM	
10 PM	

NOTES

- ☐
- ☐
- ☐
- ☐

TO-DO

- ☐
- ☐
- ☐
- ☐

DAILY PLANNER

TODAY:

Time	
8 AM	
9 AM	
10 AM	
11 AM	
12 NOON	
1 PM	
2 PM	
3 PM	
4 PM	
5 PM	
6 PM	
7 PM	
8 PM	
9 PM	
10 PM	

NOTES

- ☐
- ☐
- ☐
- ☐

TO-DO

- ☐
- ☐
- ☐
- ☐

WEEKLY PLANNER

M	
T	
W	
Th	
F	
Sa	
S	

GOALS

NOTES

REMINDER

WEEKLY PLANNER

M	
T	
W	
Th	
F	
Sa	
S	

GOALS

NOTES

REMINDER

YEARLY PLANNER

JANUARY	FEBRUARY	MARCH

APRIL	MAY	JUNE

JULY	AUGUST	SEPTEMBER

OCTOBER	NOVEMBER	DECEMBER

YEARLY PLANNER

JANUARY

....
....
....
....

FEBRUARY

....
....
....
....

MARCH

....
....
....
....

APRIL

....
....
....
....

MAY

....
....
....
....

JUNE

....
....
....
....

JULY

....
....
....
....

AUGUST

....
....
....
....

SEPTEMBER

....
....
....
....

OCTOBER

....
....
....
....

NOVEMBER

....
....
....
....

DECEMBER

....
....
....
....

www.ingramcontent.com/pod-product-compliance
Lightning Source LLC
Chambersburg PA
CBHW052343210326
41597CB00037B/6242

9 7 8 1 7 3 9 5 7 3 0 2 7